W9-CKI-362

Ferocious SHARKS

Gareth Stevens
Publishing

Please visit our Web site www.garethstevens.com. For a free color catalog
of all our high-quality books, call toll free 1-800-542-2595 or fax 1-877-542-2596.

Library of Congress Cataloging-in-Publication Data
Jackson, Tom, 1972-
 Ferocious sharks / Tom Jackson.
    p. cm. — (Dangerous animals)
 Includes index.
 ISBN 978-1-4339-4044-6 (pbk.)
 ISBN 978-1-4339-4045-3 (6-pack)
 ISBN 978-1-4339-4043-9 (library binding)
 1. Sharks—Juvenile literature. I. Title.
 QL638.9.J33 2011
 597.3—dc22

                        2010005857

Published in 2011 by
Gareth Stevens Publishing
111 East 14th Street, Suite 349
New York, NY 10003

© 2011 The Brown Reference Group Ltd.

For Gareth Stevens Publishing:
Art Direction: Haley Harasymiw
Editorial Direction: Kerri O'Donnell

For The Brown Reference Group Ltd:
Editorial Director: Lindsey Lowe
Managing Editor: Tim Harris
Editor: Tom Jackson
Children's Publisher: Anne O'Daly
Design Manager: David Poole
Designer: Aki Nakayama
Picture Manager: Sophie Mortimer
Production Director: Alastair Gourlay

Picture Credits:
Front Cover: Mary Evans Picture Library

Corbis: W. A. Raymondk: 17; istockphoto: 7b, 29bl; Henrick: 36; Hulton Archive; 8, 14;
Timeflight: 35; Jupiter Images: Photos.com: 5, 9, 11b, 13, 15t, 16, 18, 19, 23b, 25, 26, 27i,
29t , 30-31, 31 b, 32, 33, 34b, 37, 38b, 39b, 40, 41, 43, 44, 45t; Stockxpert: 7t, 10, 11t, 15b,
21, 22, 34t, 42, 45b; Shutterstock: Concettina D' Agnese

All Artworks Brown Reference Group

Printed in the United States of America
1 2 3 4 5 6 7 8 9 12 11 10

CPSIA compliance information: Batch #CS10GS: For further information contact Gareth Stevens, New York, New York at 1-800-542-2595.

CONTENTS

Any words that appear in the text in **bold** are explained in the glossary.

A shark is a fierce fish with a mouthful of sharp teeth, right? Well, that's only half the story. Many sharks are dangerous killing machines— but there are plenty of others that are not!

Sharks come in all sizes, from very small to absolutely huge. The deep-water spined pygmy shark grows to about 7 inches (18 cm)—not much longer than your hand. The largest shark of all is 70 times this size. The whale shark grows to about 40 feet (12 m), which is as long as a school bus!

SHARK ?

Most sharks live far out to sea or in shallow waters near coasts and **coral reefs**. They have an amazing set of sensors for finding **prey**. Their ears can pick up sounds coming from more than a mile (1.6 km) away. There are also small, hair-lined pits on a shark's snout that detect tiny bursts of electricity given out by prey. Special **pores** running along the side of a shark's body pick up the ripples made in the water by other animals. Sharks also have an excellent sense of smell— they can sniff the blood of a wounded animal from 0.3 miles (0.5 km) away.

UP CLOSE

Many sharks give birth to their young. Others lay eggs in cases called mermaids' purses (above). The cases are tough enough to survive being smashed against rocks on the **seabed**.

At Risk!

Very few people are killed by sharks, but people kill millions of sharks each year. Sharks are fished for their meat and for the oil in their livers, which is made into soap. The skins are made into purses and handbags. Today, most shark species are endangered.

This sand tiger shark has rows of sharp, spiky teeth. Like many other sharks, it may be killed and its teeth used to make jewelry.

ANGEL SHARK

The angel shark is named for its fins—they look a little like wings! Yet this shark is a devil in disguise, armed with lightning-fast jaws and lots of pointed teeth ready to snatch its prey.

Angel sharks spend most of their time hidden in the sand on the seabed. Like all fish, the sharks take in **oxygen** from the water. To avoid breathing in sand, angel sharks have special **gill slits**, called **spiracles**. These are on the tops of their heads and stick out of the sand. By pumping water through the spiracles, the sharks can keep still while breathing—and stay hidden from their prey.

Tail

Dorsal fin

Pectoral fin, or "wing"

Spiracle

Eye

Hidden Danger!

The angel shark likes to rest on the seabed, with its body buried and just the eyes on the top of the head showing. Although the shark keeps very still, it is always ready to grab prey with its strong jaws.

UP CLOSE

An angel shark's mottled skin provides excellent camouflage as it lurks on the seabed. An angel shark cannot swim fast but waits for prey to come close. Then, the shark lunges.

Common name: angel shark
Scientific name: Squatina squatina
Size: can grow up to 8 ft (2.4 m) long
Key features: flat body with winglike pectoral fins; small thorns on snout
Diet: flatfish, rays, and skates; crabs, lobsters, and squid

BASKING

With its vast, gaping jaws, the basking shark looks truly scary. Incredibly, its mouth is big enough for a person to fit inside!

Well Named!

As its name suggests, the basking shark likes to float near the warm surface of the sea—often with its back out of the water—as if the shark were "basking" in the sunshine.

The basking shark is found all over the world's oceans. It does not hunt prey but eats huge amounts of tiny creatures called **plankton**, which live near the surface of the ocean. It takes food from the water using vast **gill rakers**. In one hour, a basking shark takes in enough water to fill an Olympic-sized swimming pool!

Tail

Dorsal fin

Pectoral fin

Gills

SHARK

Common name: basking shark

Scientific name: Cetorhinus maximus

Size: usually around 33 ft (10 m), but may be up to 50 ft (15 m)

Key features: huge mouth; skin covered in thick layer of smelly, slimy **mucus**; 5 gill slits with gill rakers for filtering food

Diet: plankton

UP CLOSE

A basking shark has about 600 tiny teeth in its upper jaw and 800 in the lower one! But basking sharks don't bite. Instead, they eat by taking in great gulps of water.

BULL SHARK

Shark Eat Shark!

Adult bull sharks eat almost anything, including other sharks. They prey on young lemon sharks, hammerheads, and dog sharks—and even eat baby bull sharks!

The bull shark is the world's most dangerous shark. It lives close to the coast and often attacks people swimming or wading in shallow, muddy water.

The bull shark lives in warm, **tropical** oceans. It prefers shallow water, including coral reefs and **estuaries**. This shark has even been seen up the Amazon River, 2,600 miles (4,200 km) from the ocean! However, the bull shark is not always the biggest hunter around. It is sometimes attacked by crocodiles in the Nile River.

Tail

Dorsal fin

Pectoral fin

Gills

Huge mouth

10

UP CLOSE

A bull shark's huge mouth allows the shark to tackle some surprising prey. The shark attacks hippopotamuses in the slow-flowing waters of African rivers, as well as antelope and cattle.

Common name: bull shark
Scientific name: *Carcharhinus leucas*
Size: usually less than 11.5 ft (3.5 m)
Key features: stout, sturdy body; blunt head with broad snout; saw-edged teeth in upper jaw
Diet: eats almost anything—turtles, prawns, lobsters, sea urchins, squid, and octopus

DOGFISH

Dogfish are the most common of all sharks. They are fast swimmers and grab fish and other animals with their sharp teeth before gulping them down.

These sharks are called dogfish because they have a rounded snout, like a dog's. However, to confuse things a little, the dogfish is actually a member of the cat shark family! Dogfish live in the eastern Atlantic Ocean and Mediterranean Sea.

Gills

Dorsal fin

Tail

Pectoral fin

Spotted body

Common name: dogfish
Scientific name: Scyliorhinus canicula
Size: up to around 4 ft (1.2 m), but usually smaller
Key features: slim body and slightly flattened head; large dark eyes and mouth set back from tip of snout
Diet: whelks and clams; prawns and crabs; seahorses, flatfish, worms, and sea cucumbers

Lurking Low!

The dogfish lurks at the bottom of shallow water, where it usually rests during daylight hours. The fish often hides among rocks. As darkness falls, it sets out in search of food.

UP CLOSE

A dogfish's face is rounded like a dog's snout. But its eyes are like those of a cat!

GREAT WH

The great white shark is a perfect hunting machine! Its massive body speeds through the water and overpowers prey with a huge bite.

The great white uses all its senses to track its prey. The shark listens for the sounds made by prey, then it sniffs it out. A great white could smell a single drop of blood in a swimming pool! The shark sees well in deep, dark water and usually attacks from below. At first, it takes a quick bite. If it likes the taste, the shark comes back for the rest.

UP CLOSE

Great whites have between 12,000 and 30,000 teeth during their lifetime. The teeth are arranged in rows that work like a conveyor belt. As one tooth wears out, another slides into place.

Dorsal fin

Gray upper body

Tail

Teeth

Gills

Pale underside

TE SHARK

Common name: great white shark

Scientific name: Carcharodon carcharias

Size: can grow up to 20 ft (6 m)

Key features: torpedo-shaped body; sharp, saw-edged teeth; gray and white skin

Diet: fish, including other sharks, turtles, seabirds, dolphins, seals, and sea lions

SHARK ATTACK!

Shark attacks make headlines around the world. Around 100 people are attacked each year, but only about ten of them die. You are more likely to die from a bee sting than a shark attack!

15

HAMMERHEAD SHARK

Hammerheads are the weirdest looking sharks of all. The wide, T-shaped head works like a scanner to find food buried in sand.

If one hammerhead looks amazing, imagine what a group of 200 hammerheads looks like! Scalloped hammerheads (the most common type) swim in these large gangs. The sharks gather to find mates and protect themselves against predators, such as killer whales.

UP CLOSE

A hammerhead has an eye at each end of its "hammer." That allows the shark to look on both sides at once. However, it can't see straight ahead. It must sweep its head from side to side to check what's in front.

In The Tropics!

Many hammerheads live in tropical regions. Some swim in the warm, shallow waters around coral reefs, while others prefer the deeper waters of the open sea.

EAD

"Hammer" (head)

Tail

Eye

Dorsal fin

Gills

Pectoral fin

Common name: hammerhead shark

Scientific name: Sphyrnidae

Size: from 3 ft (90 cm) to around 20 ft (6 m)

Key features: T-shaped head, with eyes and nostrils located on the ends of lobes; powerful, muscled body

Diet: squid, shellfish, sea snakes, bony fish, skates, rays, other sharks, squid, and shellfish

17

LONGNOSE

The longnose sawshark has a supersnout edged with toothlike spikes. Female sawsharks give birth to their young. The babies are born with their spikes folded backward so they don't hurt their moms.

The longnose sawshark uses its snout to find and then catch prey. Pores on the snout pick up the electrical signals given out by other animals, even if they are buried in the sand or mud. Two long whiskers called barbels hang from the shark's jaw. The shark drags its whiskers along the ocean floor to pick up the taste of food buried there.

UP CLOSE

The longnose sawshark uses its snout to uncover animals that are buried in the sand. It swipes its snout from side to side to stun the prey. Then the shark bites its victim with rows of sharp, pointed teeth.

SAWSHARK

Common name: longnose sawshark
Scientific name: *Pristiophorus cirratus*
Size: can grow up to 54 in (137 cm) long
Key features: long snout; long, slender body; brown or grayish brown on top, white underside
Diet: mostly eats small fish, squid, and **crustaceans**

Deep Down!

The longnose sawshark lives on the sandy or muddy bottom of the ocean floor. It lives so deep down that it rarely comes into contact with people, so it is not likely to hurt anyone.

Snout

Dorsal fin

Tail

Barbel

Pectoral fin

MEGAMOU
SHARK

A s its name suggests, the megamouth shark has a huge mouth. But not a lot more is known about this giant shark because it swims in the dark waters far, far below the surface.

Until 1976, no one knew that the megamouth shark even existed! But in November of that year, a U.S. Navy research vessel caught a 14.6-foot (4.5-m) shark. No one had ever seen anything like it. This was a historic event because the shark was a new **species**. Since then, megamouths have been found in the Atlantic, Indian, and Pacific Oceans.

Tail

Dorsal fin

Pectoral fin

Gills

On The Move!

Megamouths live at different depths in the sea at different times of the day. They spend the day up to 500 feet (150 m) below the surface. As it gets dark, the sharks travel upward, following the shrimp and fish they eat.

UP CLOSE

It is dark in deep water. The megamouth's huge mouth glows in the dark. This may help the shark attract prey. Small squid are drawn toward the shark's bright mouth.

Common name: megamouth shark
Scientific name: Megachasma pelagios
Size: largest known female measured 17 ft (5.2 m); males probably smaller
Key features: huge, rounded head with short snout; enormous mouth with tiny teeth
Diet: mostly shrimp, jellyfish, and other **invertebrates**

NURSE SHA

The nurse shark may grow to be longer than a car, and it has a big appetite. This shark eats mostly other fish, including dangerous stingrays. Sometimes it will swallow a sea snake. Don't go too close: They do bite!

Nurse sharks are named for the slurping noises they make when they are eating. This sound reminds people of the sounds made by a nursing baby.

Resting Together!

Nurse sharks hunt at night and spend the day resting in groups on the seafloor, piled on top of each other. They like shallow water and often carpet the seabed near beaches.

RK

Tail

Dorsal fin

Gills

Pectoral fin

Barbel

UP CLOSE

Hanging down from the nurse shark's lower jaw are a pair of thin, fleshy whiskers, called barbels. These are sensitive to touch and taste. The shark uses the barbels to find food.

Common name: nurse shark
Scientific name: *Ginglymostoma cirratum*
Size: around 14 ft (4.3 m); females are slightly larger than males
Key features: gray upper body, white on underside; sloping forehead and short, downward-facing mouth
Diet: bottom-dwelling fish, crabs, lobsters, and octopuses

THRESHER SHARK

Almost half of a thresher shark's body is made up of its long, pointed tail. The tail makes the shark a graceful swimmer, but also a ruthless killer!

A group of thresher sharks use their long, flexible tails to round up **schools** of fish such as mackerel, herring, or sardines. The sharks swim in smaller and smaller circles, forcing their prey to crowd together. The sharks then slap the fish with their tail **fins**. This stuns the fish and makes them easier to catch.

UP CLOSE

The thresher shark's tail is divided into two parts, or lobes. The upper lobe is the long part. It can be almost as long as the rest of the shark's body.

Common name: thresher shark
Scientific name: Alopiidae
Size: can grow up to 20 ft (6 m) long
Key features: strong, muscular body; upper part of tail as long as body; gray or black on top with white belly
Diet: mainly fish (including herring, mackerel, and sardines), squid, and crustaceans such as crabs

At The Surface!

Thresher sharks mostly swim near the surface of the water and stay away from coasts. They are strong swimmers and can even leap out of the water. Some kinds can dive to great depths—as deep as 1,640 ft (500 m).

Dorsal fin

Upper lobe of tail

Lower lobe

Pectoral fin

White belly

25

TIGER SH

The tiger shark is one of the deadliest sharks of all. With its strong jaws and sharp, jagged teeth, it will try to eat just about anything—including people!

The tiger shark's nickname could be "the garbage can with fins." A tiger shark will eat almost anything—turtles, seabirds, seals, whales, dolphins, cats, and donkeys have all been on its menu. The tiger shark also swallows plenty of less tasty stuff, too, including glass bottles, tin cans, rubber tires, sacks of coal, and even dynamite!

Dorsal fin

Tail

Jagged teeth

Pectoral fin

...ARK

Common name: tiger shark
Scientific name: *Galeocerdo cuvier*
Size: 10-14 ft (3-4.3 m) long
Key features: broad, blunt snout; large mouth with huge, saw-edged teeth
Diet: eats anything edible; also swallows many other things, such as cloth, bits of metal, and rubber tires

Shark Attack!

Some other sharks may attack people more often, but tiger sharks kill more people than any other shark species. The tiger shark rips chunks off its prey from the first bite. There are no pauses between bites, so there is little chance of escape.

UP CLOSE

The tiger shark gets its name from the dark bars on its body. They look like the pattern on a tiger. The pattern is strongest on young tiger sharks and fades as the sharks get older.

WHALE SH

The whale shark is the biggest fish in the sea. It weighs 15 tons (13,600 kg), which is heavier than three elephants! It is a filter feeder, sucking tiny fish and plankton into its huge mouth. Divers should be careful near a whale shark, since the powerful tail can cause serious injury.

The whale shark has a pattern of spots and stripes on its back. Each one has its own unique pattern—like a fingerprint. The shark swims by swaying its body from side to side. It moves about as quickly as a person walks. In spite of its great size, the whale shark is under threat. People hunt it for its meat, which is cut into strips and then dried in the sun.

Old Giants!

Whale sharks can live to be 70 years old. They spend their lives in warm oceans, swimming in the open sea.

ARK

Dorsal fin

Tail

Gill slits

Pectoral fin

Common name: whale shark
Scientific name: Rhincodon typus
Length: up to 40 ft (12 m)
Key features: whalelike body with massive, flat head; enormous gaping mouth with lots of tiny teeth
Diet: plankton, small fish, and other small animals filtered out by gill rakers

UP CLOSE

A whale shark has a lot of teeth—about 3,000 of them! But the teeth (below) are only tiny, and the shark does not use them to bite or catch its food.

GLOSSARY

camouflage A coloring or body shape that helps an animal blend with and hide in its surroundings.

coral reef A line of coral that lies below the water in warm, shallow seas. Coral is made up of tiny animals.

crustacean An animal with a tough outer shell. Most crustaceans—including lobsters, crabs, and shrimp—live in water.

dorsal fin The triangular-shaped fin on the back of a shark's body. It helps the shark balance as it swims.

estuaries Places where freshwater, such as a river, meets the tide.

fins The winglike parts that stick out from a shark's body. They help the shark swim and balance.

gill rakers Bony parts that sift out food from water passing through the gills of the shark.

gill slits Slits in a shark's body that allow it to breathe underwater. The gills take in oxygen from the water.

invertebrate An animal without a backbone (spine).

mucus A thick, slippery fluid used to protect body parts.

oxygen A gas that animals must breathe to survive.

pectoral fin One of a pair of fins that lie just behind a shark's head. The pectoral fins help a shark control direction as it swims.

plankton Tiny animals and other creatures that live near the surface of the ocean.

pore A small opening in an animal's skin.

predator An animal that hunts other animals for food.

prey An animal that is hunted by another animal.

school A large group of fish.

seabed The sandy or muddy bottom of the sea.

species A group of animals that share features. Members of the same species can mate and produce young together.

spiracles Small gill slits just behind a shark's head.

tropical The hot parts of Earth nearest to the equator. The equator is an imaginary line around the middle of Earth.

FURTHER RESOURCES

Books about sharks

Dubkowski, Cathy East. Shark Attack! New York: DK Children's Books, 2009.

Nuzzolo, Deborah. Tiger Shark. Mankato, MN: Capstone Press, 2008.

O'Donnell, Kerri. Hammerhead Sharks. New York: PowerKids Press, 2006.

Randolph, Joanne. The Great White Shark: King of the Ocean. New York: PowerKids Press, 2007.

Useful Web sites

Facts About Sharks
http://www.sharks-world.com/

National Geographic Kids: Great White Sharks
http://kids.nationalgeographic.com/Animals/CreatureFeature/Great-white-shark

Shark Facts and Pictures
http://cybersleuth-kids.com/sleuth/Science/Animals/Mammals/Marine__Mammals/Sharks/index.htm

Sharks
http://www.kidzone.ws/sharks/

Publisher's note to educators and parents: Our editors have carefully reviewed these Web sites to ensure that they are suitable for students. Many Web sites change frequently, however, and we cannot guarantee that a site's future contents will continue to meet our high standards of quality and educational value. Be advised that students should be closely supervised whenever they access the Internet.

INDEX